# Bo and Zop
## learn how to be an
# EARTHLING

# HOW DO EARTHLINGS GET ALONG?

## by Kirsty Holmes

**CRABTREE**
PUBLISHING COMPANY

**Author:** Kirsty Holmes

**Editorial director:** Kathy Middleton

**Editors:** Madeline Tyler, Janine Deschenes

**Proofreader:** Melissa Boyce

**Graphic design:** Dan Scas

**Production coordinator
 & Prepress technician:** Ken Wright

**Print coordinator:** Katherine Berti

**Images**

All images are courtesy of Shutterstock.com, unless otherwise specified.

Alien Bo: delcarmat. Alien Zop: Roi and Roi. Background – PremiumArt. Vectors throughout: kearia.

Speech bubbles: Surrphoto.

All facts, statistics, web addresses and URLs in this book were verified as valid and accurate at time of writing. No responsibility for any changes to external websites or references can be accepted by either the author or publisher.

**Library and Achives Canada Cataloguing in Publication**

Title: How do earthlings get along? / Kirsty Holmes.
Other titles: Getting along
Names: Holmes, Kirsty, author.
Description: Series statement: Bo & Zop learn how to be an earthling |
 Originally published under title: Getting along: a book about peace. King's
 Lynn: BookLife, 2020. | Includes index.
Identifiers: Canadiana (print) 20200225383 |
 Canadiana (ebook) 20200225391 |
 ISBN 9780778781189 (hardcover) |
 ISBN 9780778781226 (softcover) |
 ISBN 9781427125682 (HTML)
Subjects: LCSH: Interpersonal relations—Juvenile literature. |
 LCSH: Peace-building—Juvenile literature. | LCSH: Conflict management—
 Juvenile literature. | LCSH: Conduct of life—Juvenile literature.
Classification: LCC HM1126 .H65 2021 | DDC j303.6/9—dc23

**Library of Congress Cataloging-in-Publication Data**

Names: Holmes, Kirsty, author.
Title: How do earthlings get along? / Kirsty Holmes.
Description: New York : Crabtree Publishing Company, [2020] |
 Series: Bo & Zop learn how to be an earthling | Includes index.
Identifiers: LCCN 2020016374 (print) | LCCN 2020016375 (ebook) |
 ISBN 9780778781189 (hardcover) |
 ISBN 9780778781226 (paperback) |
 ISBN 9781427125682 (ebook)
Subjects: LCSH: Interpersonal conflict--Juvenile literature. |
 Social conflict--Juvneile literature. | Interpersonal relations--
 Juvenile literature. | International relations--Juvenile literature. |
 Conflict management--Juvenile literature.
Classification: LCC HM1121 .H65 2020 (print) | LCC HM1121 (ebook) |
 DDC 302--dc23
LC record available at https://lccn.loc.gov/2020016374
LC ebook record available at https://lccn.loc.gov/2020016375

# Crabtree Publishing Company

www.crabtreebooks.com          1-800-387-7650

**Published by Crabtree Publishing Company in 2021**

Printed in the U.S.A./072020/CG20200429

**Published in Canada
Crabtree Publishing**
616 Welland Avenue
St. Catharines, Ontario
L2M 5V6

**Published in the United States
Crabtree Publishing**
347 Fifth Ave
Suite 1402-145
New York, NY 10016

# CONTENTS

Bo and Zop learn how to be an EARTHLING

**Words with lines underneath, like <u>this</u>, can be found in the glossary on page 24.**

# SOMEWHERE IN THE SOLAR SYSTEM...

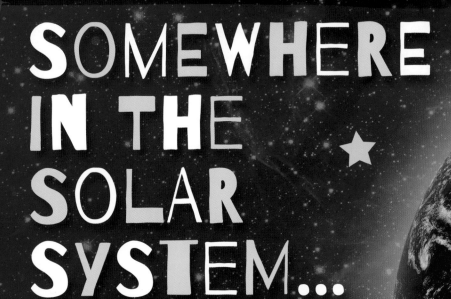

Look up into the night sky. Can you see it? One star is shining brighter than all the others. Is it a star? It could be a <u>satellite</u>. Or it could be... an alien spaceship!

Earth

Alien spaceship

Bo and Zop have been in this spaceship for a long time. It is a very long way from Omegatron, and it is a very small ship.

"Get your stupid teddy bear out of my side of the ship!"

"First, get your stinky socks out of my side!"

6

Bo and Zop have started to argue. They cannot find a way to share the spaceship! Can Bo and Zop learn how to get along by studying Earthlings?

There are toys everywhere!

The sink is full of dirty dishes!

"YOUR MUSIC IS TOO LOUD!"

"I can't hear you. My music is too loud!"

# WHY DO EARTHLINGS DISAGREE?

Earthlings don't always agree. They might have different **opinions** or feelings. They might do things in different ways. Can you think of a time you disagreed with someone?

Sometimes, Earthlings disgree with the people they live with. Children might disagree with their parents about house rules. Siblings might disagree about toys, music, or who gets the last piece of cake!

"I can see that Earthlings love their family members, even when they disagree."

Earthlings also disagree with others in their local and global communities. Earthling coworkers might disagree about how a job should be done. An Earthling might argue with a friend about which game to play.

"Earthlings can live, work, and play in their communities... even when they don't agree!"

World leaders do not always agree, but many of them work together to make Earth a good place to live.

Earthlings around the world have different opinions. Some Earthlings disagree about the <u>laws</u> that a country should have. Others disagree about how the environment should be protected. The global community is a better place to live when Earthlings show <u>respect</u> to each other, even when they disagree.

# NOT GETTING ALONG

When countries cannot find a way to agree, they may fight each other in wars.

"Look, Zop. Wars hurt many Earthlings."

Sometimes, Earthlings cannot find a way to get along. They do not always show respect to those they disagree with. There can be serious effects when this happens. Earthlings could get hurt after having an argument.

Earthlings show they disagree in different ways. They might cross their arms or shake their heads. They might speak out in public. They could make art that shows their ideas. They might argue with each other.

Protesting is one way Earthlings show others that they disagree with something.

# WORKING THROUGH ARGUMENTS

Some Earthlings take a deep breath when they feel angry.

Other Earthlings walk away instead of arguing.

It is normal for Earthlings to disagree. But there are many ways that Earthlings work through arguments. Earthlings can talk through problems to find a way to agree. They can try to calm down if they are angry.

Earthlings try to learn the <u>perspectives</u> of others. Understanding perspective helps them work through arguments. It lets them see how the other Earthling thinks and feels.

"Bo, how do you feel when my music is loud?"

"I feel frustrated because I can't hear my own music."

# SAYING SORRY

Sometimes, feelings are hurt in an argument. So Earthlings know that it is important to say sorry to each other. Saying sorry helps someone know that their feelings are respected.

"Thank you, Bo. I'm sorry too. Here are your socks."

"I'm sorry I threw your bear, Zop. That must have made you feel sad. Here you go."

**Earthlings show they are sorry in many different ways.**

They say "I'm sorry."

They write apology notes.

I'm Sorry...

They do acts of kindness.

# LEARNING FROM OTHERS

Earthlings listen to others to understand their perspectives. Listening helps them find a way to agree. They take time to put themselves in others' shoes.

"Okay. I'm wearing your shoes."

"It's only a saying, Bo. It means you should try to understand someone else's perspective by imagining you are them."

"Here are some ways Earthlings show they are good listeners!"

- They give others time to speak.

- They look for good things about the other perspective.

- They think before responding.

- They politely ask questions to understand more.

- They use words and <u>body language</u> to show that they understand the different perspective.

# TIMES OF PEACE

Sharing

Waiting their turn

When Earthlings disagree, they look for a way to make both people happy. A solution that makes everyone happy is called a compromise. There are many kinds of compromises.

When Earthlings agree to a compromise, everyone gets a little bit of what they wanted, and no one is left unhappy. There is no arguing, and Earthlings can live in peace with each other.

Can you think of a time that you agreed to a compromise?

# BO AND ZOP GET ALONG

Bo and Zop have learned a lot from Earthlings about getting along. They agree it is time to share the spaceship without arguing.

Bo decides to write an apology letter to Zop. What do you think his letter should say?

"It's nice to get along."

"It's nice to say sorry too!"

Dear Zop,

Bo and Zop have learned to compromise. As long as the two aliens can get along, living in a spaceship high above Earth should be much easier!

# GLOSSARY

**body language** — Body movements, such as nods or smiles, that send a message

**Earthlings** — Human beings

**global** — Worldwide

**laws** — Rules decided by government

**local** — Relating to a certain nearby place

**opinions** — Judgments or beliefs based on personal experiences

**perspective** — Point of view: how a person sees something

**protesting** — Showing one's disagreement with something

**respect** — Viewing and treating someone or something with admiration and thoughtfulness

**satellite** — A human-made object that circles Earth or another space object

# INDEX